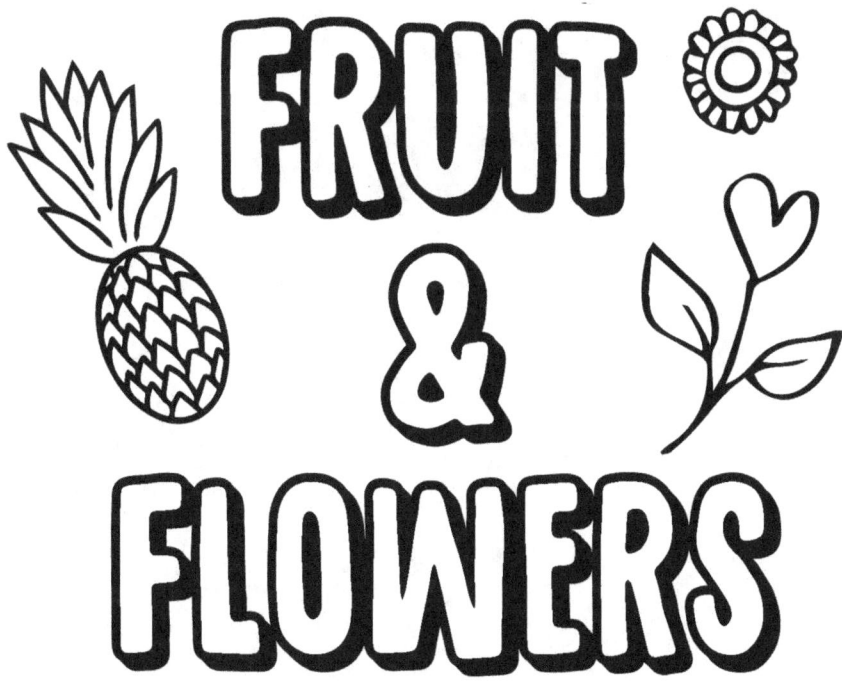

FRUIT & FLOWERS

ADULT
COLORING BOOK

by DANI KATES

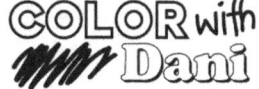
COLOR with Dani

Be Like a Pineapple

STAND TALL
Wear a Crown &
Be Sweet
ON THE INSIDE

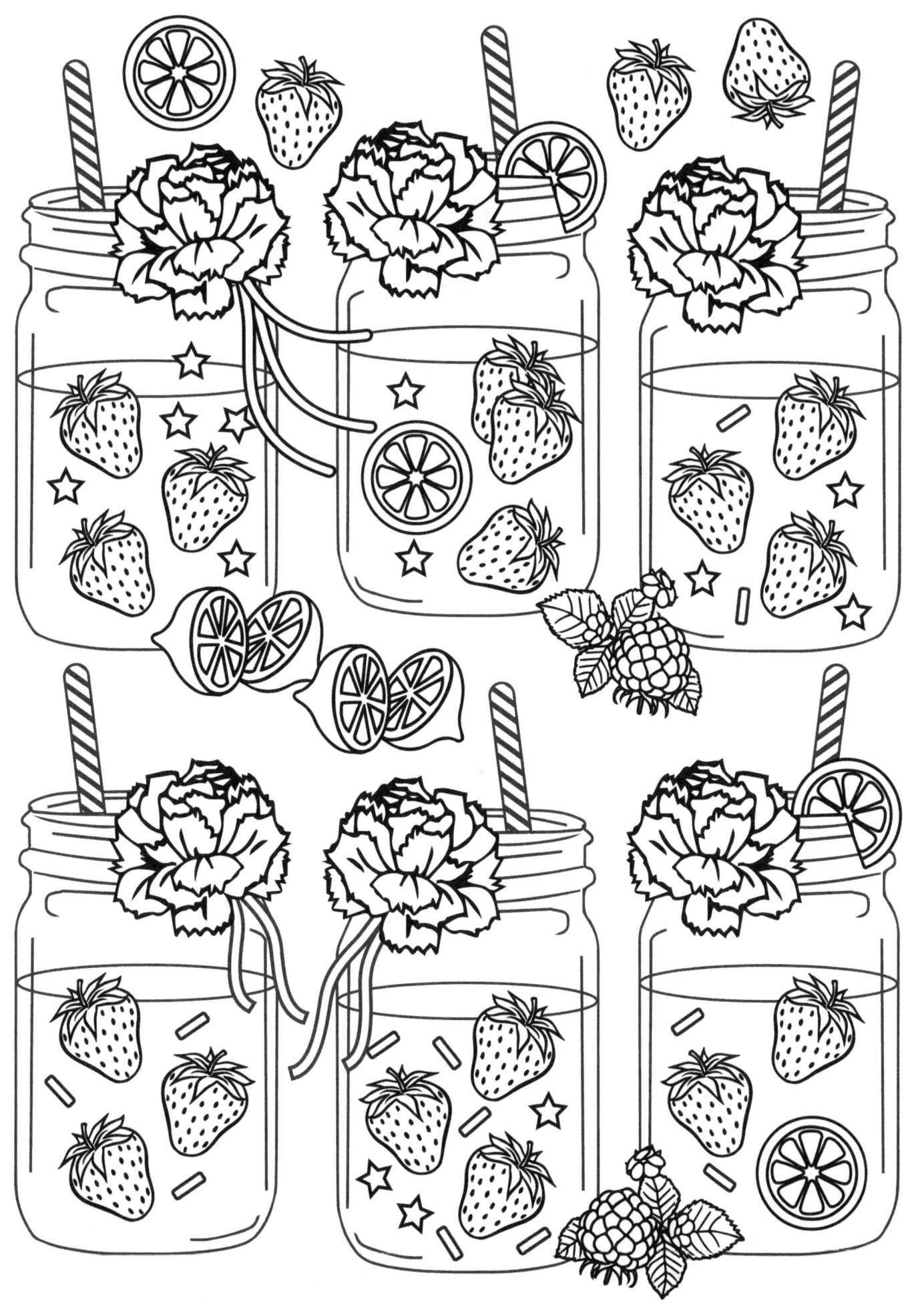

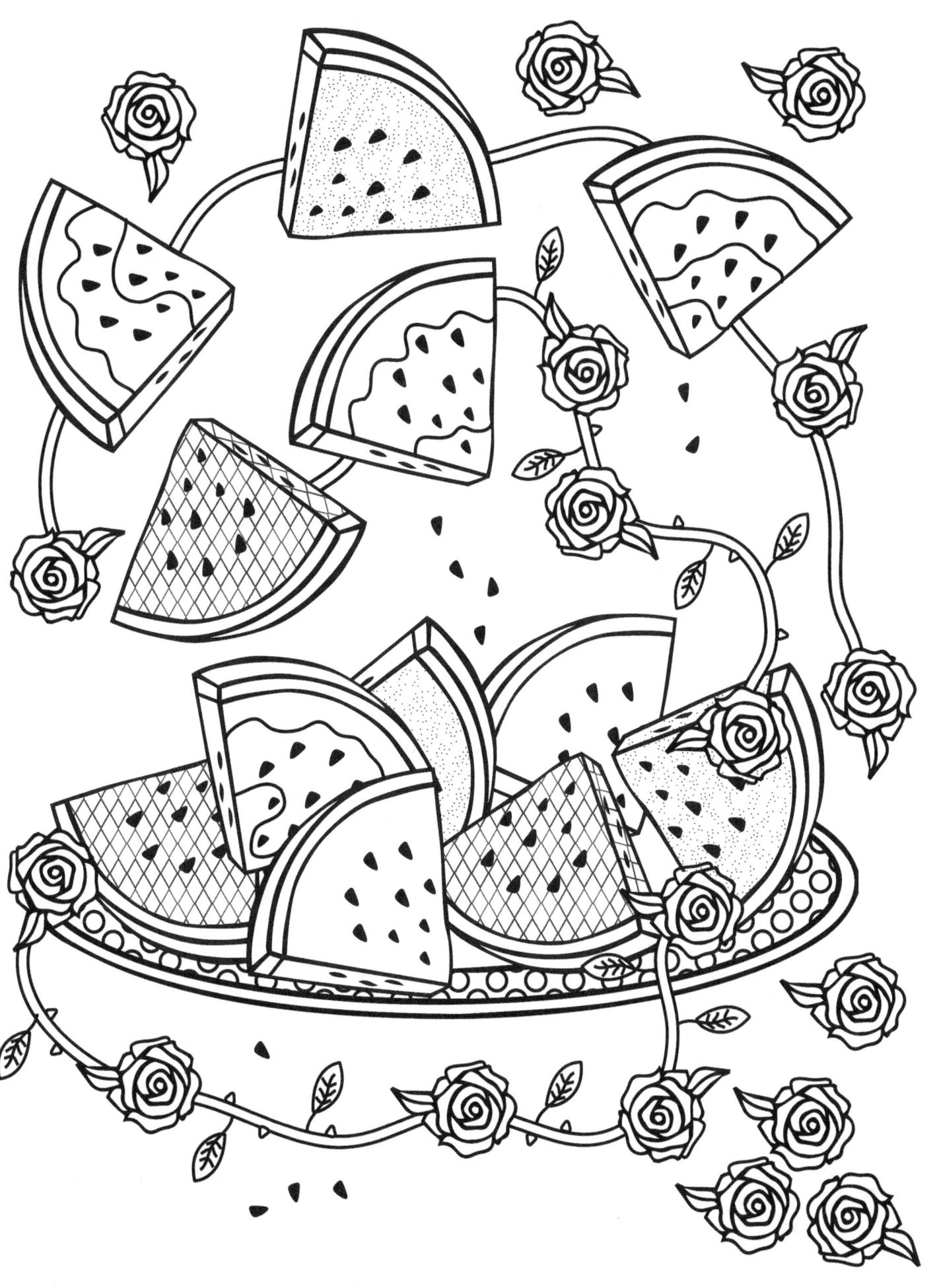

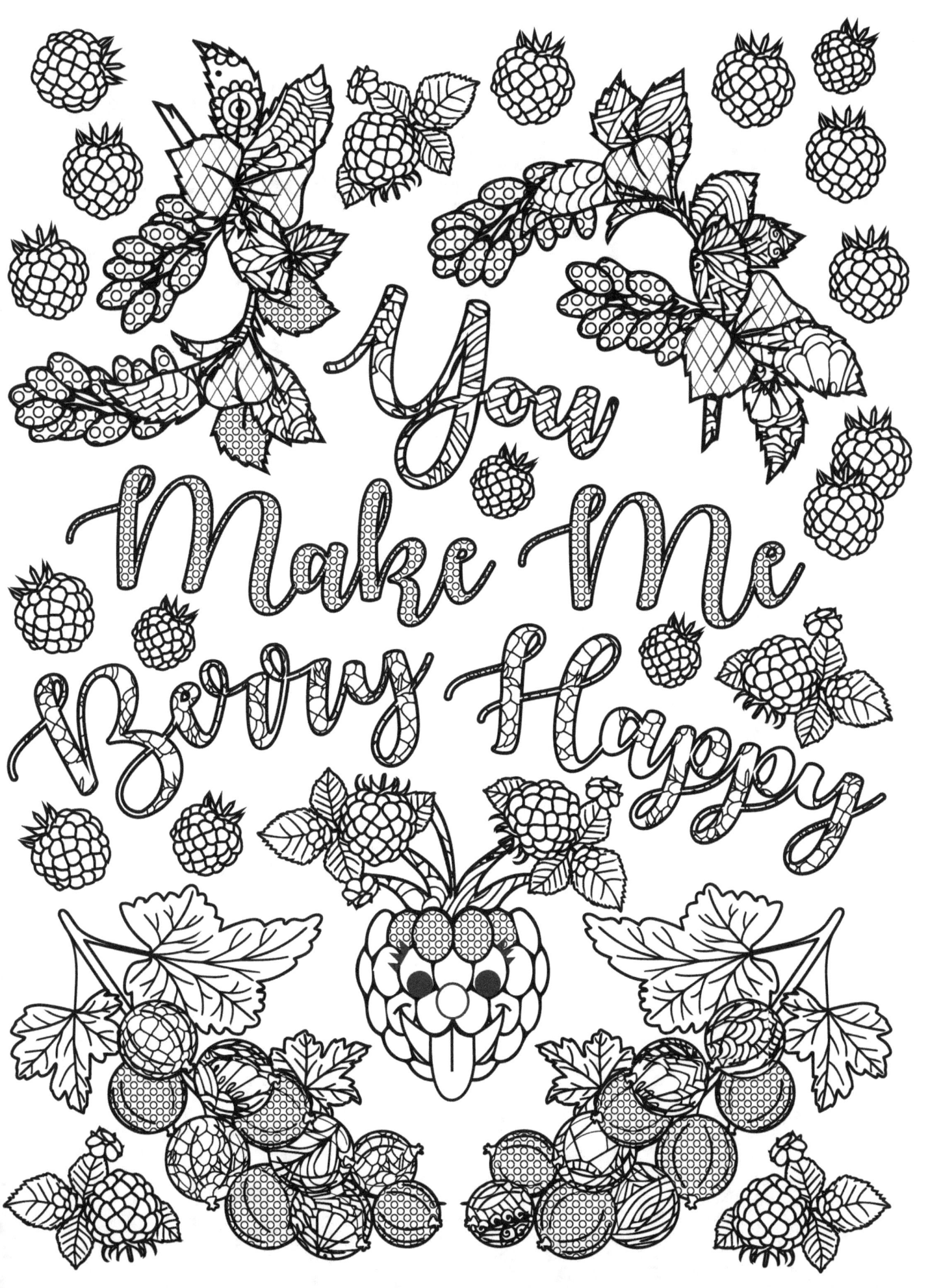

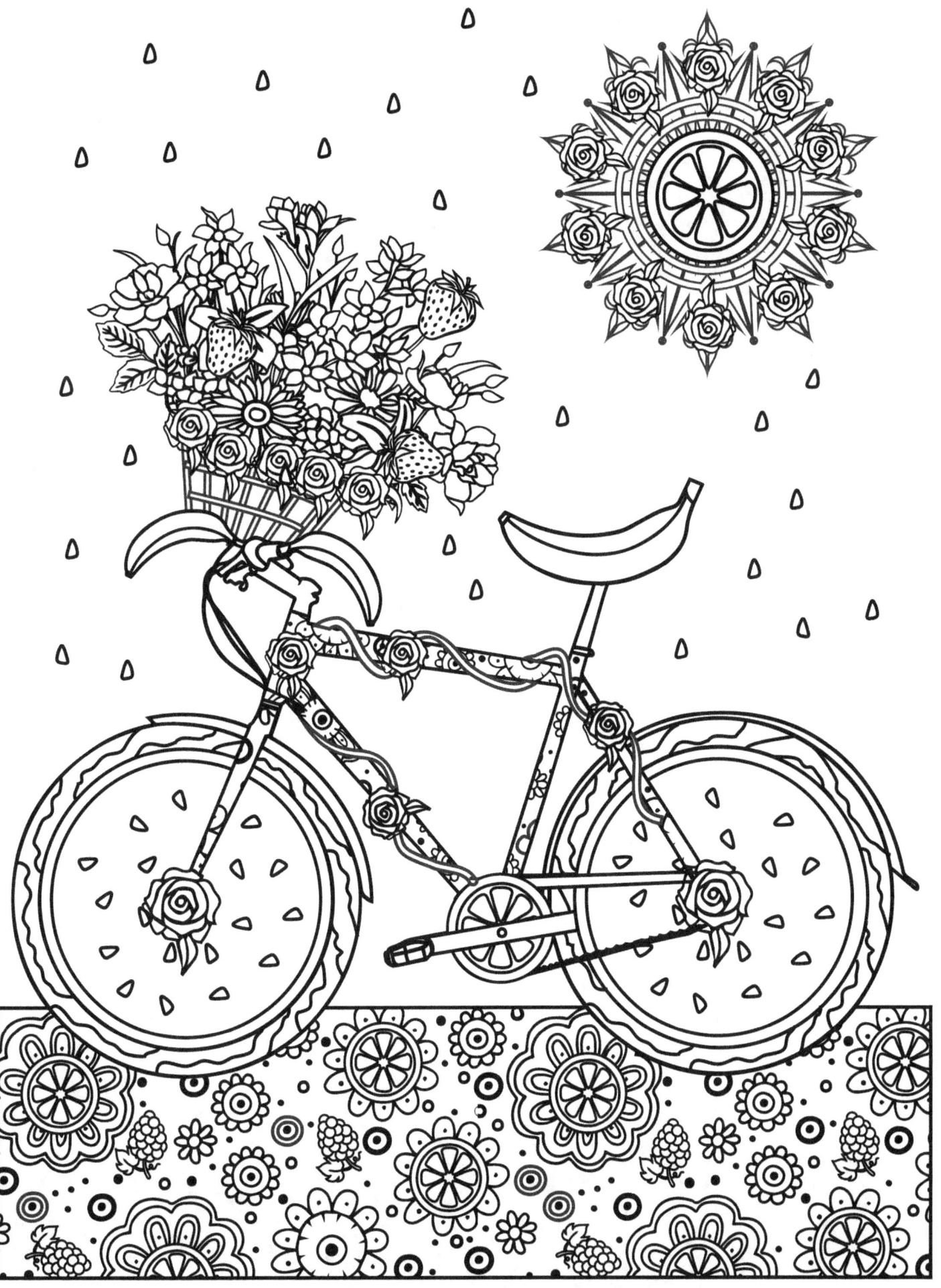

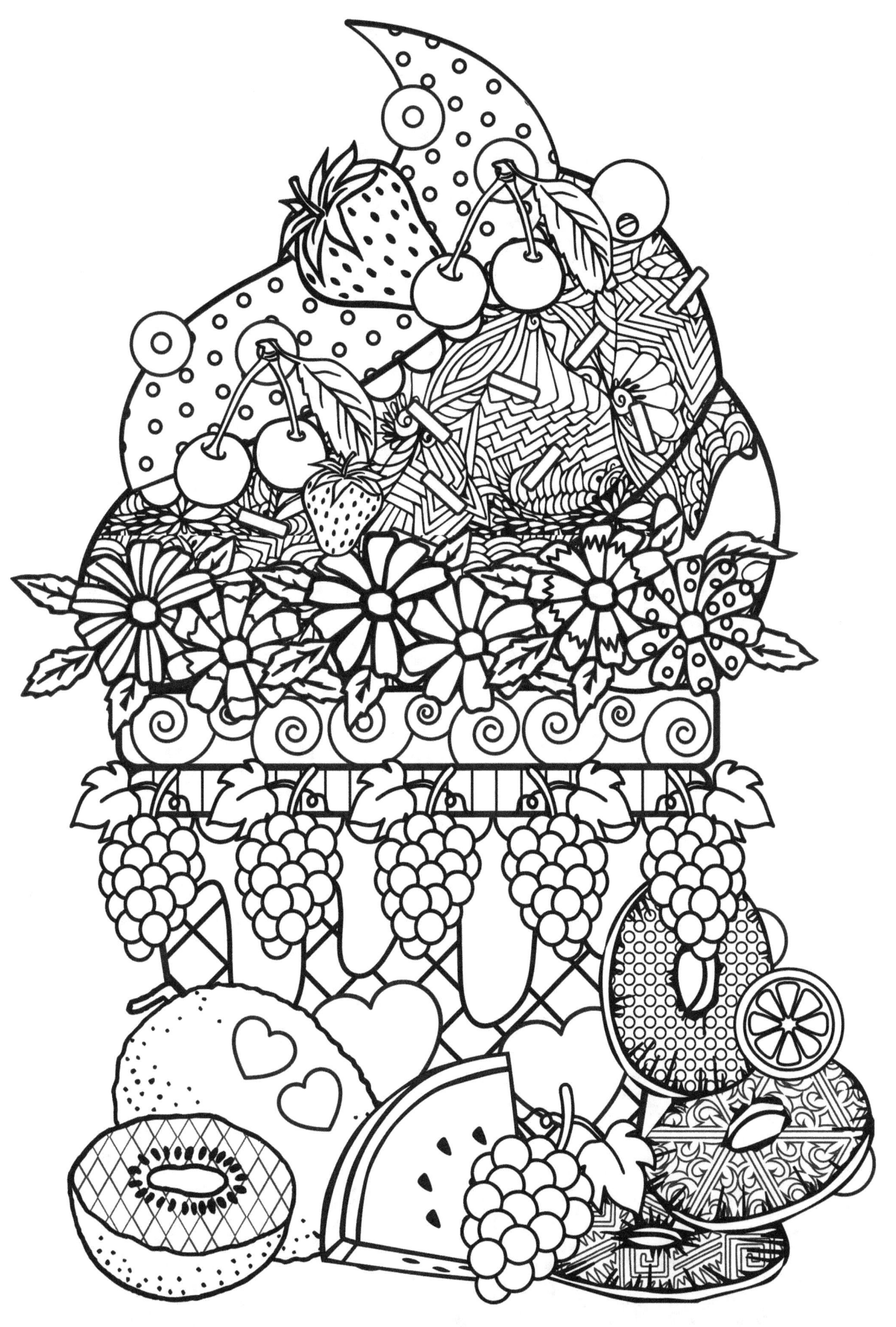

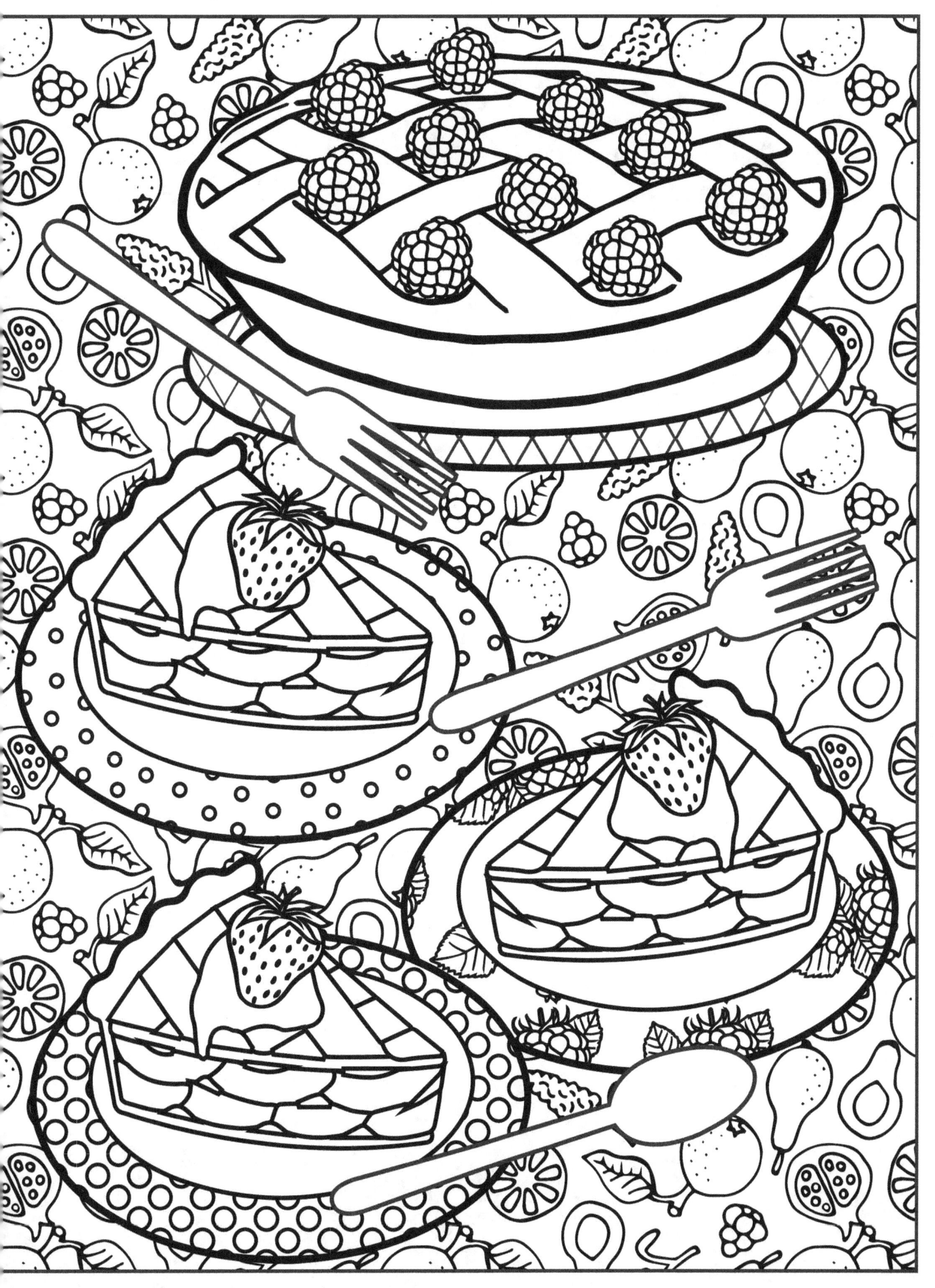

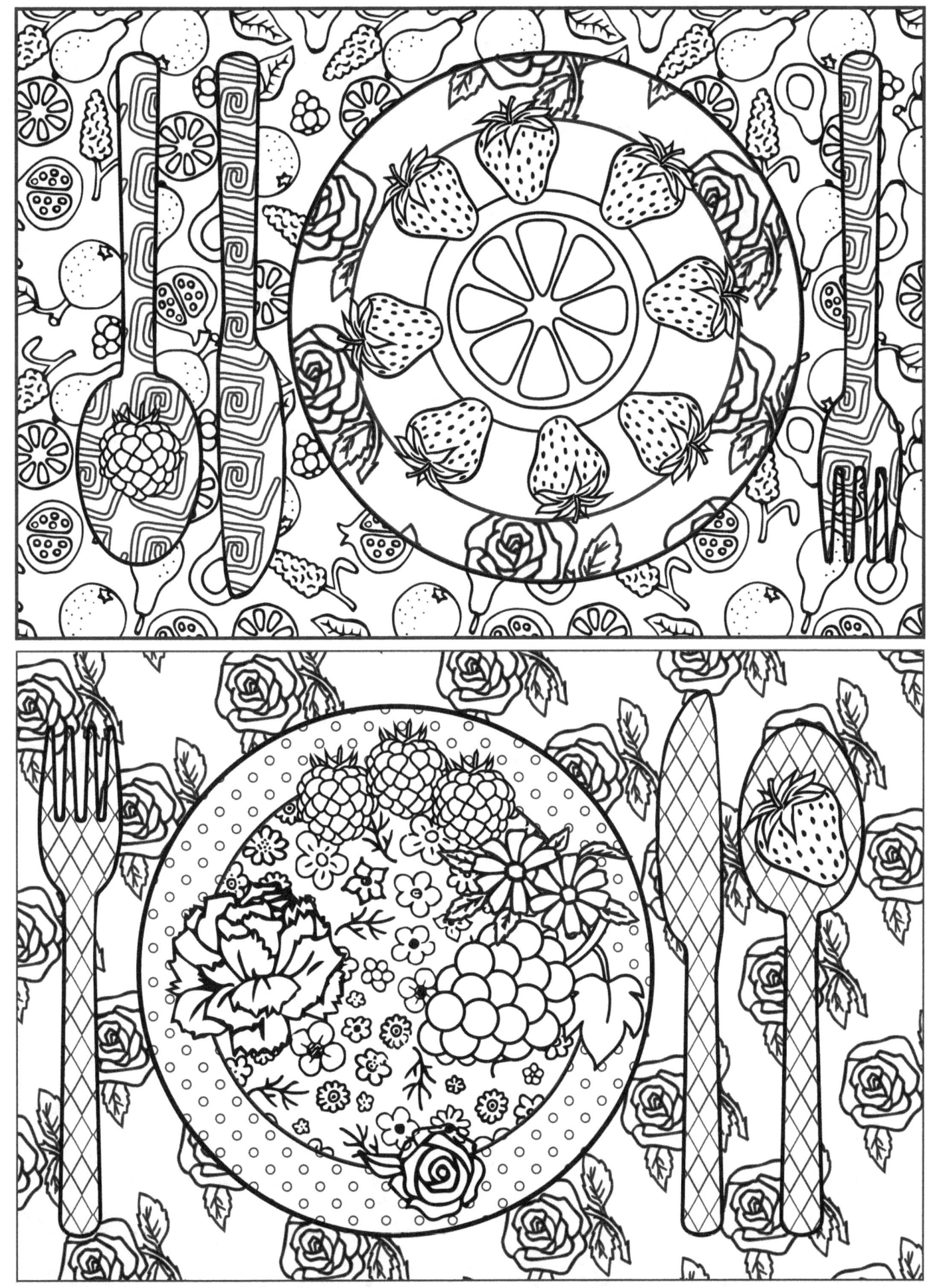

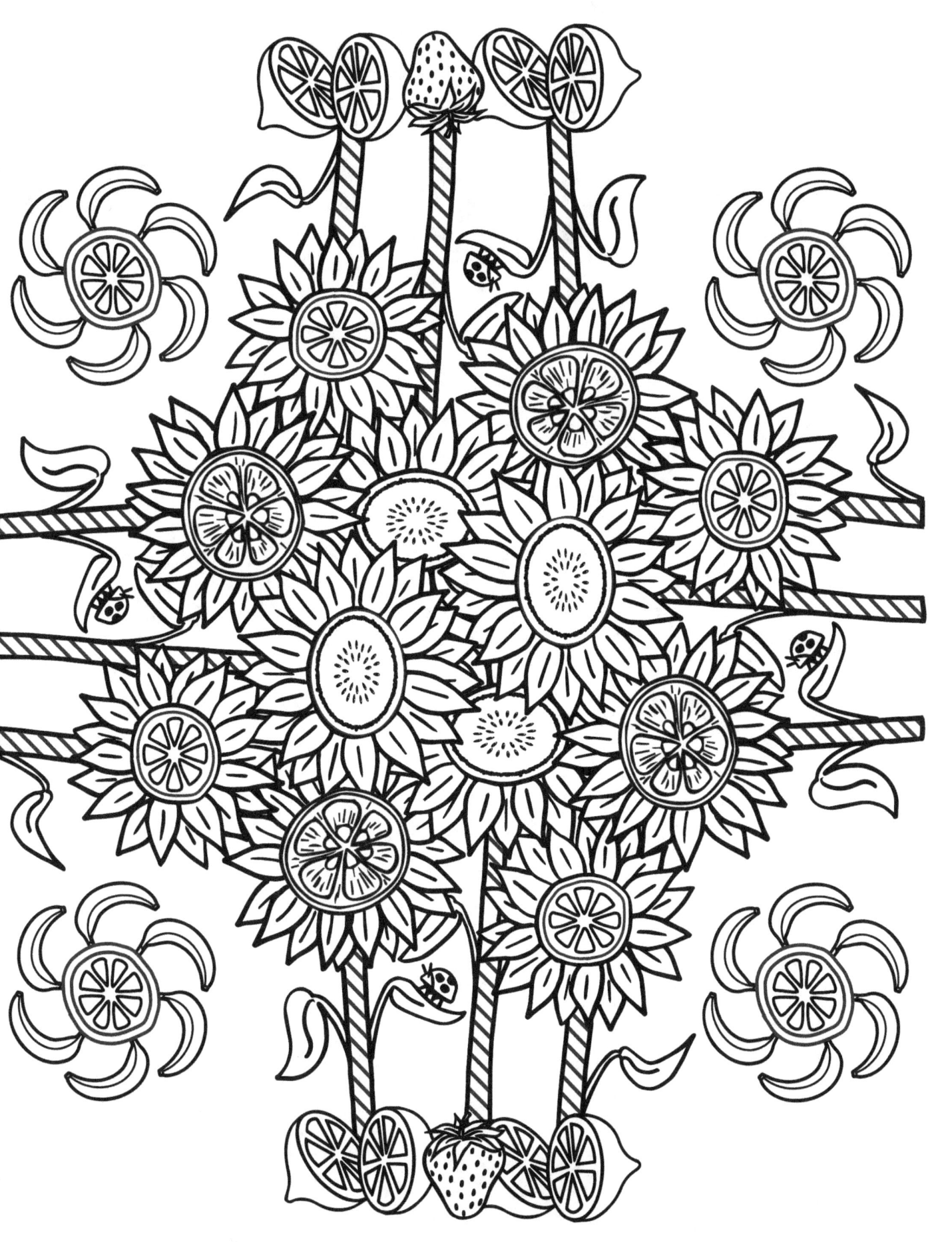

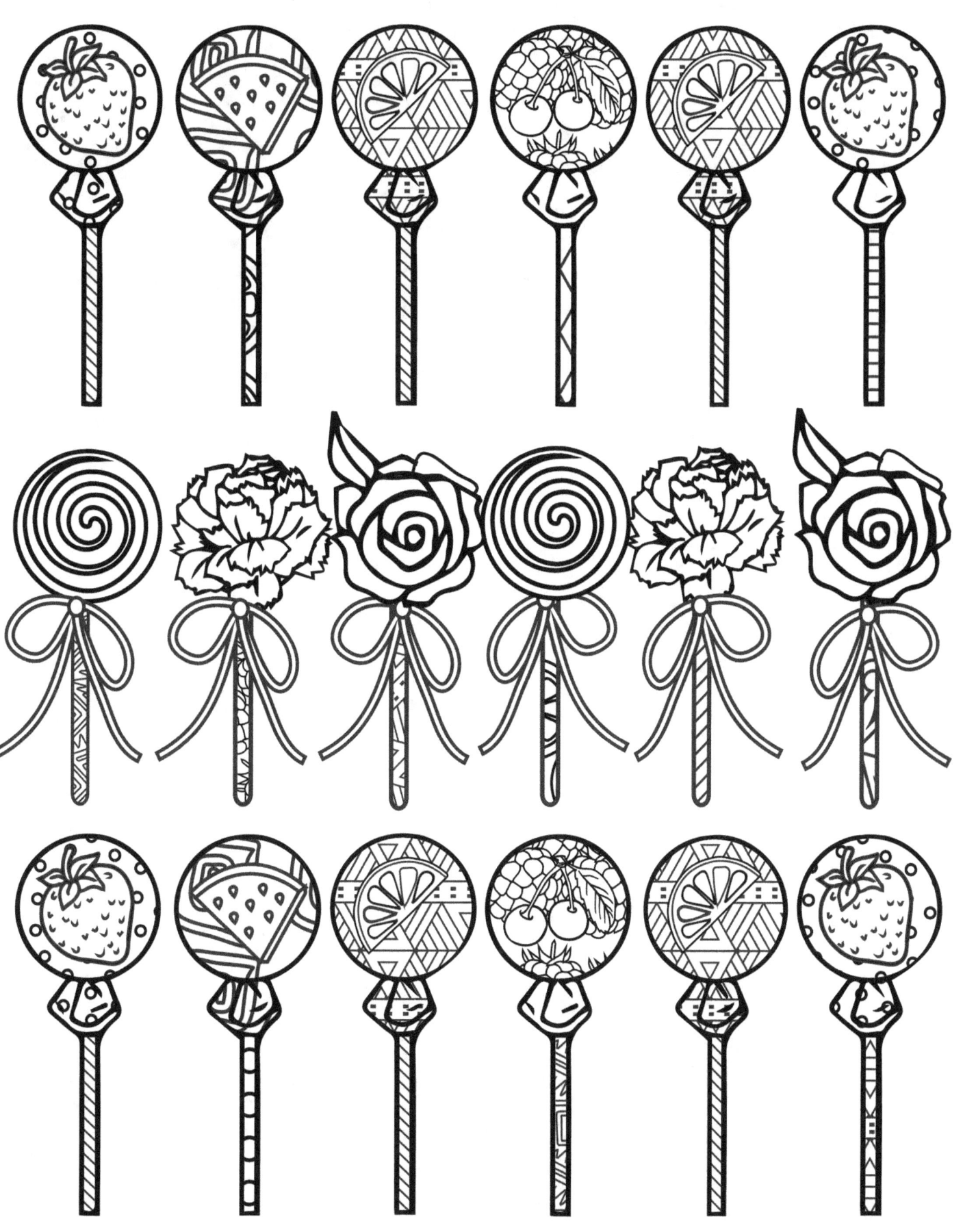

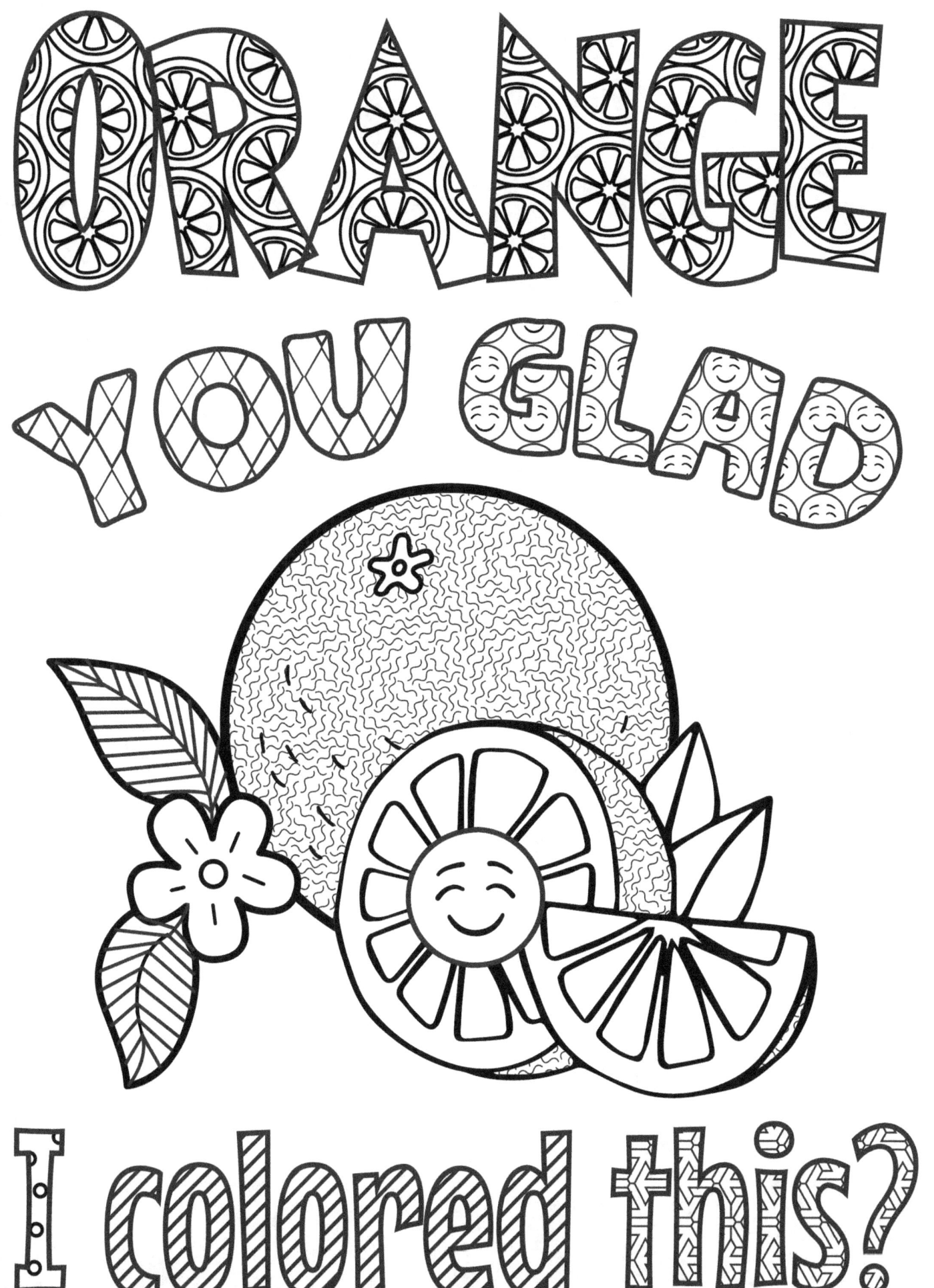

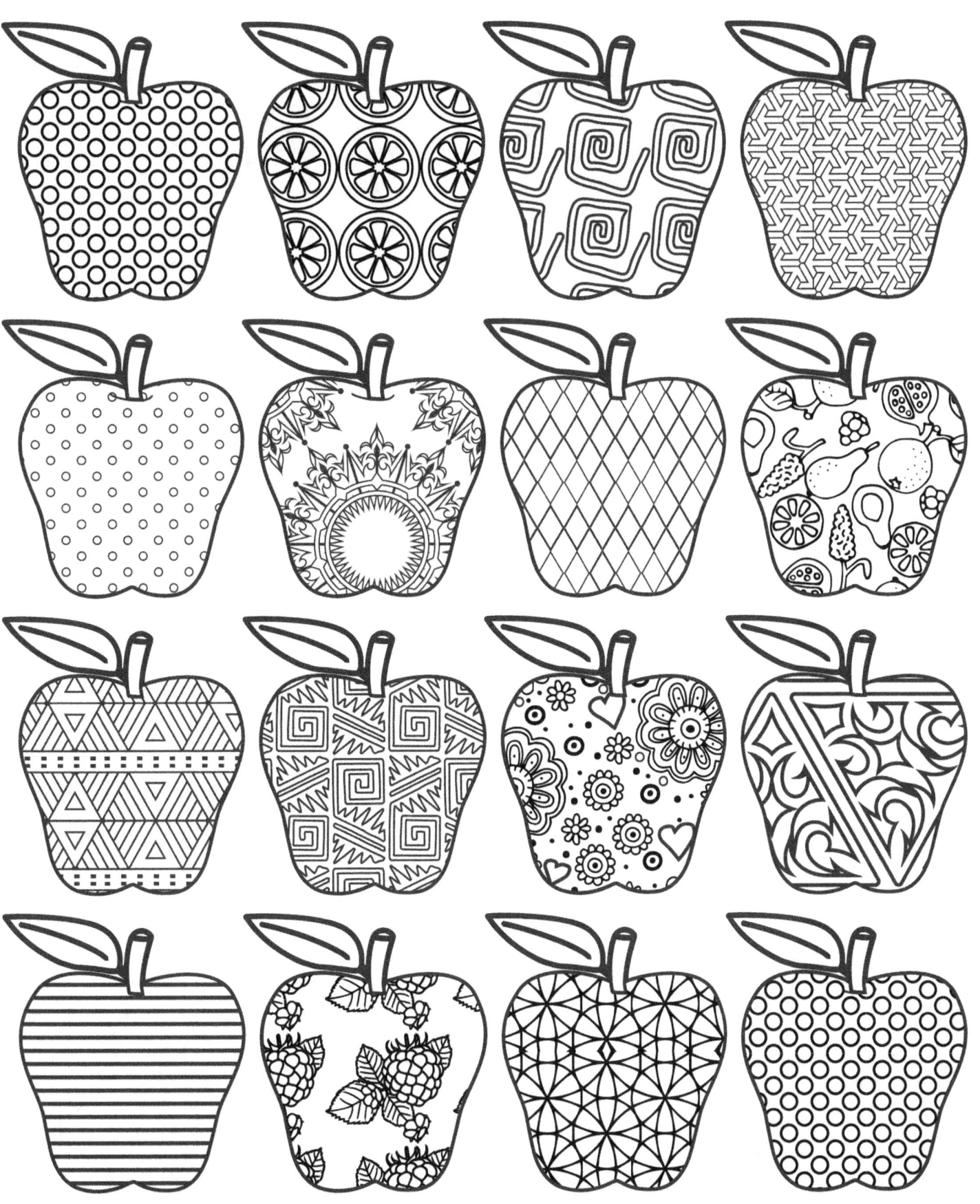

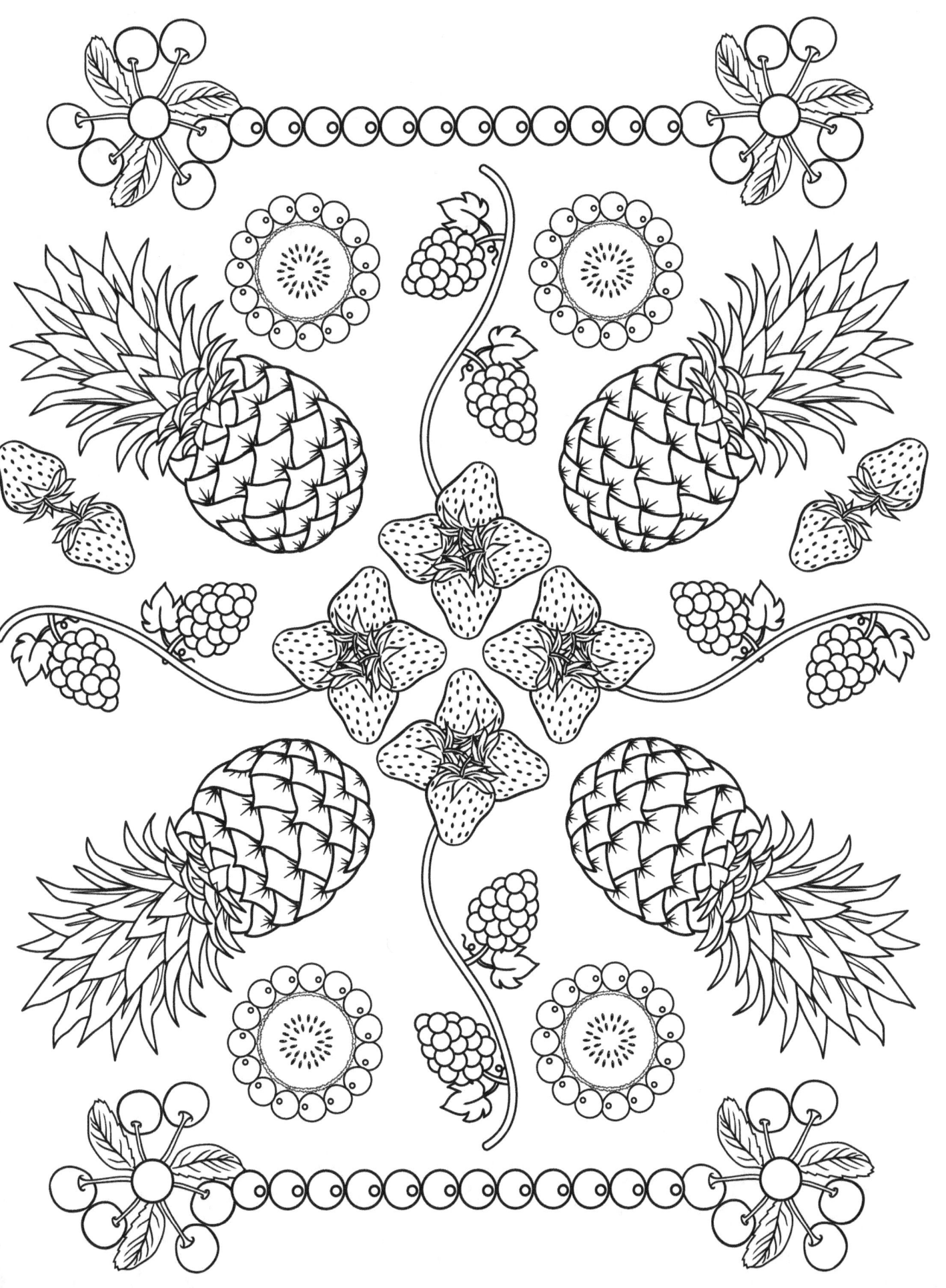

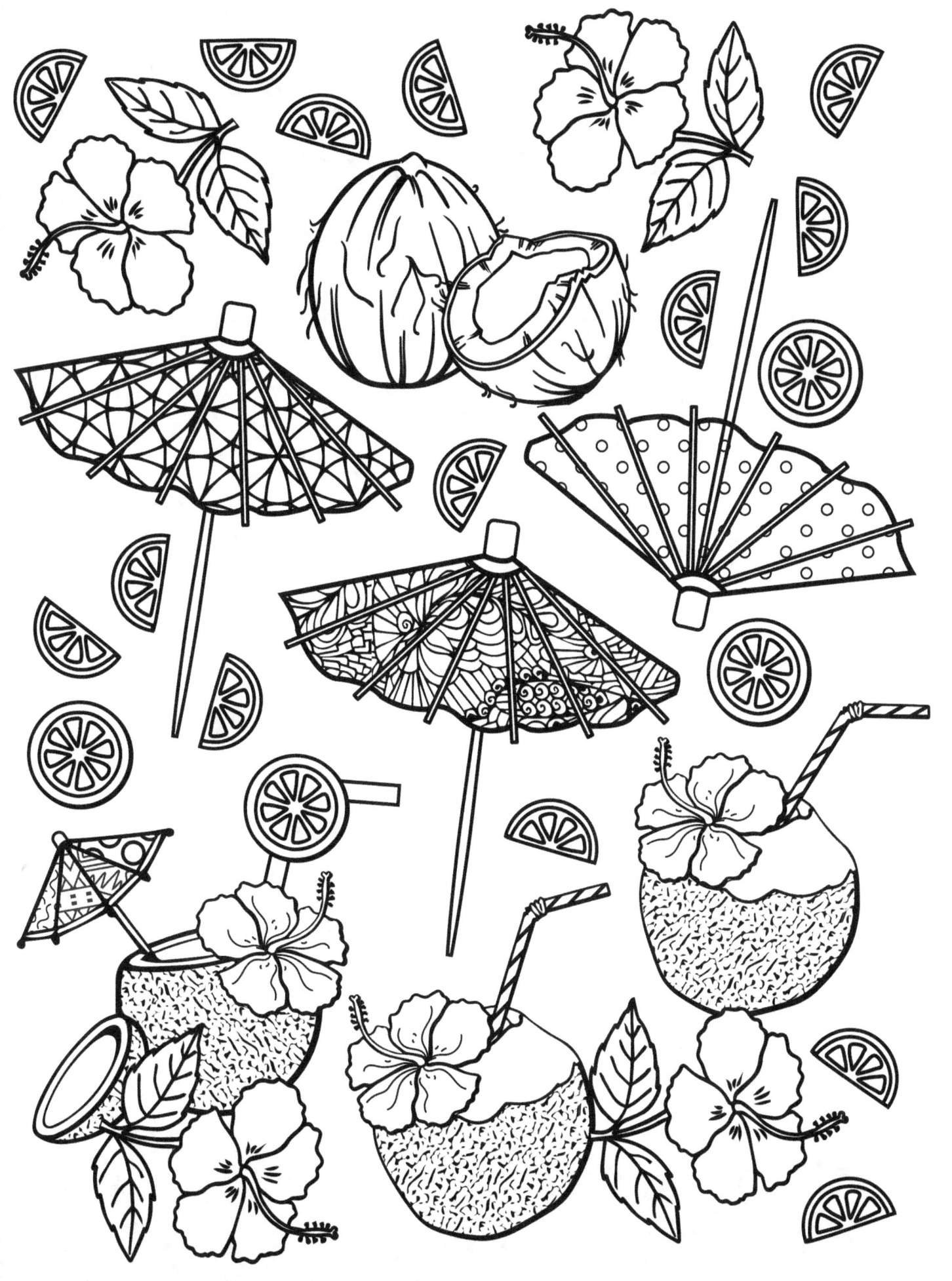

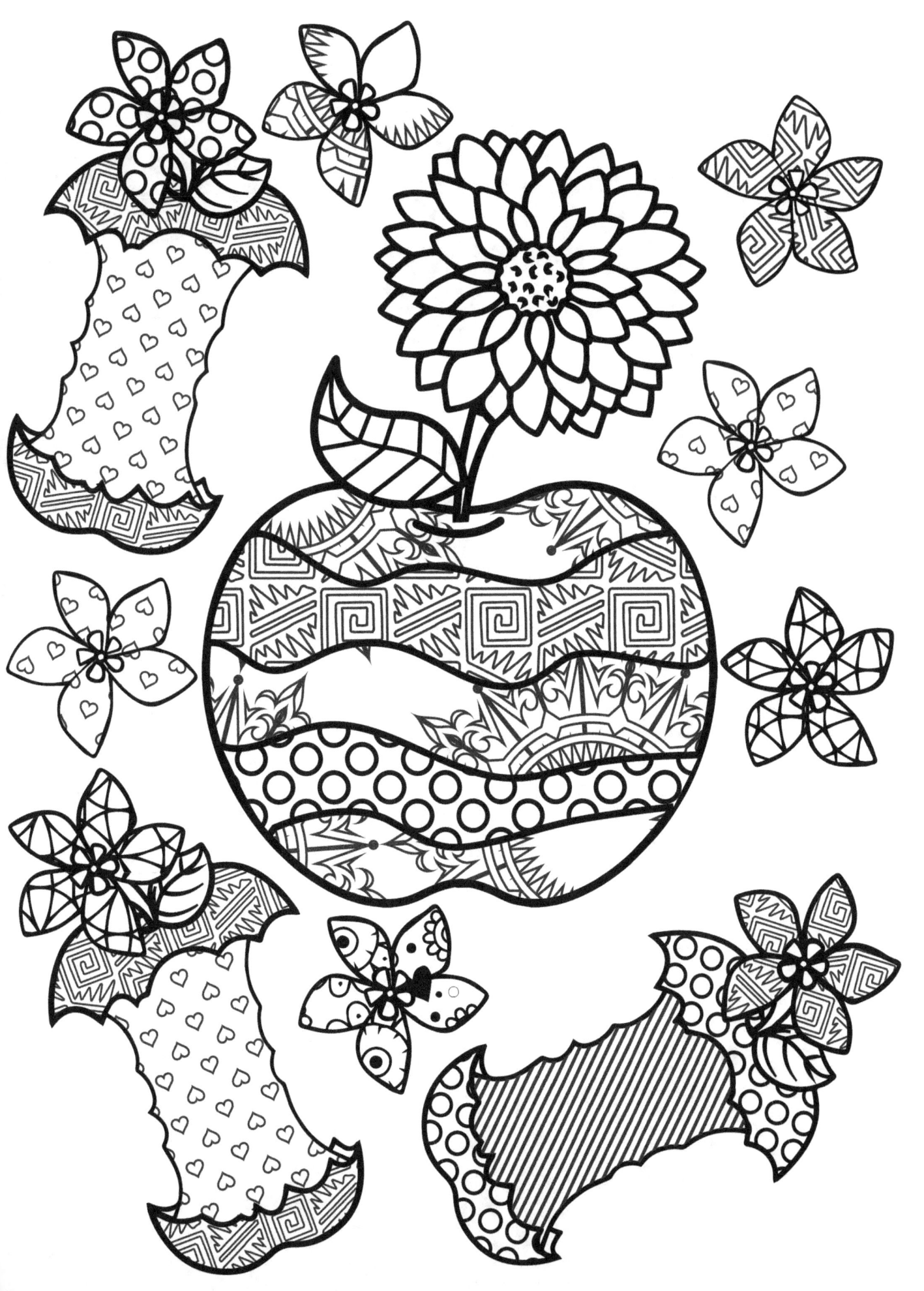

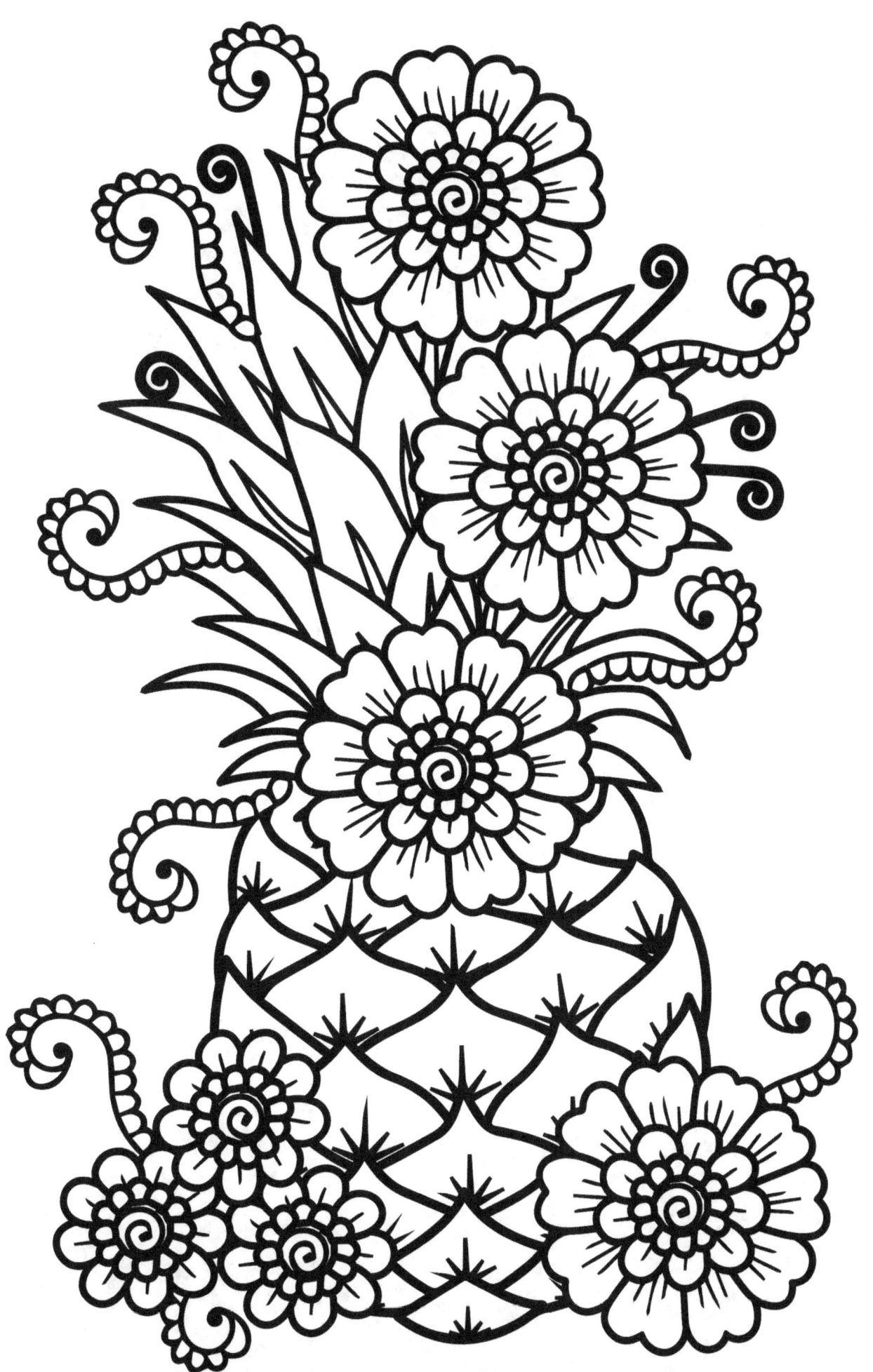

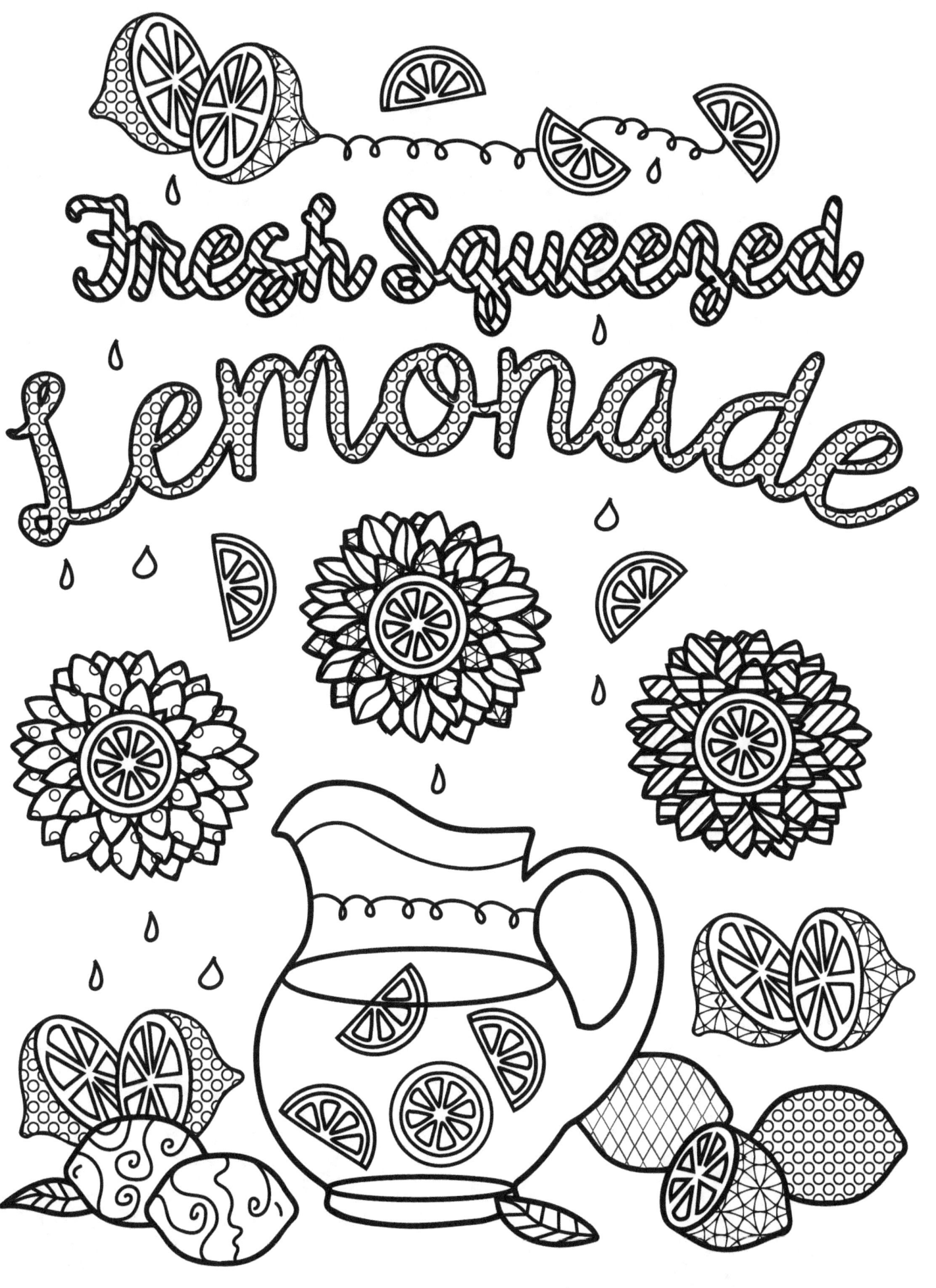

WE MAKE A GREAT PEAR

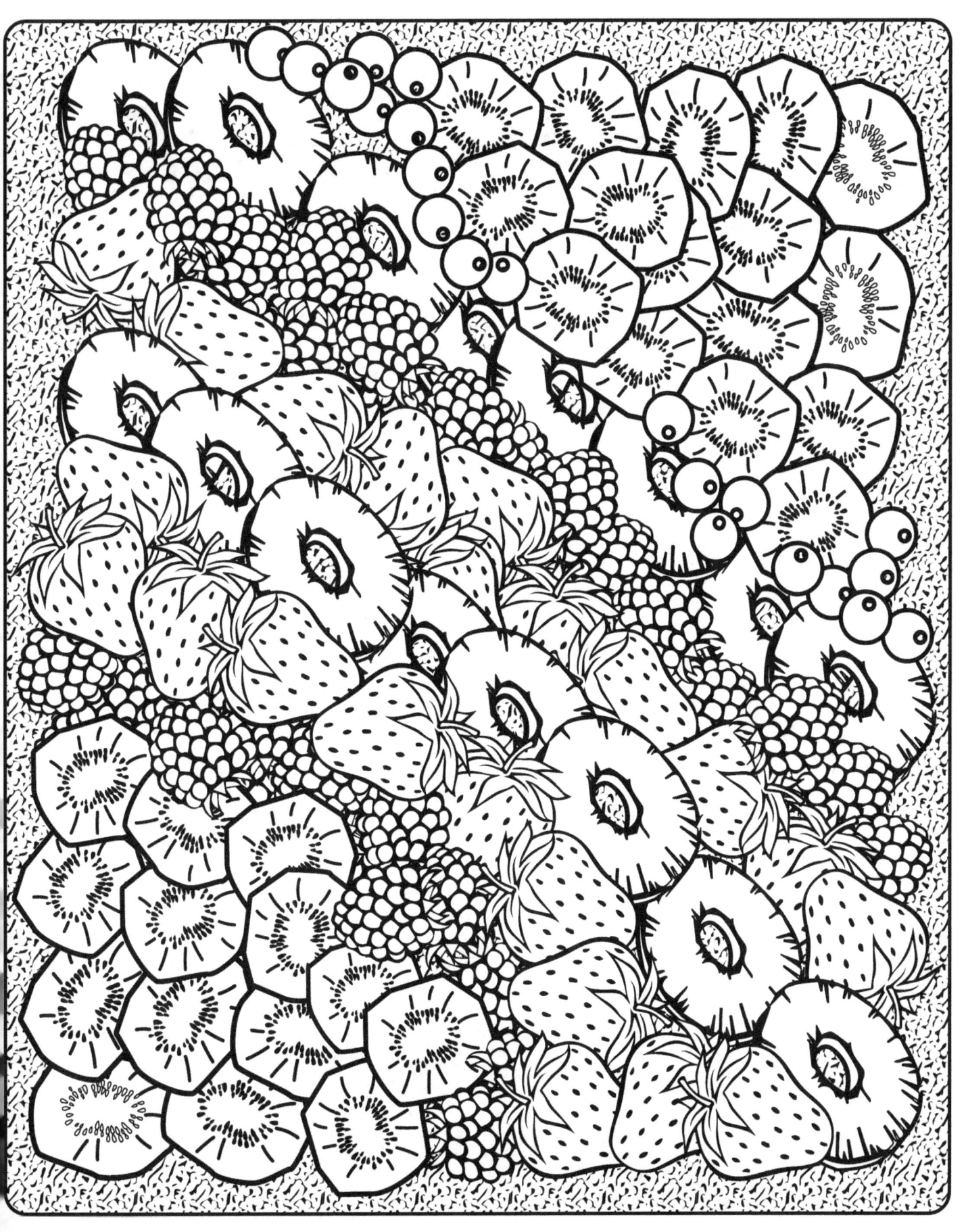

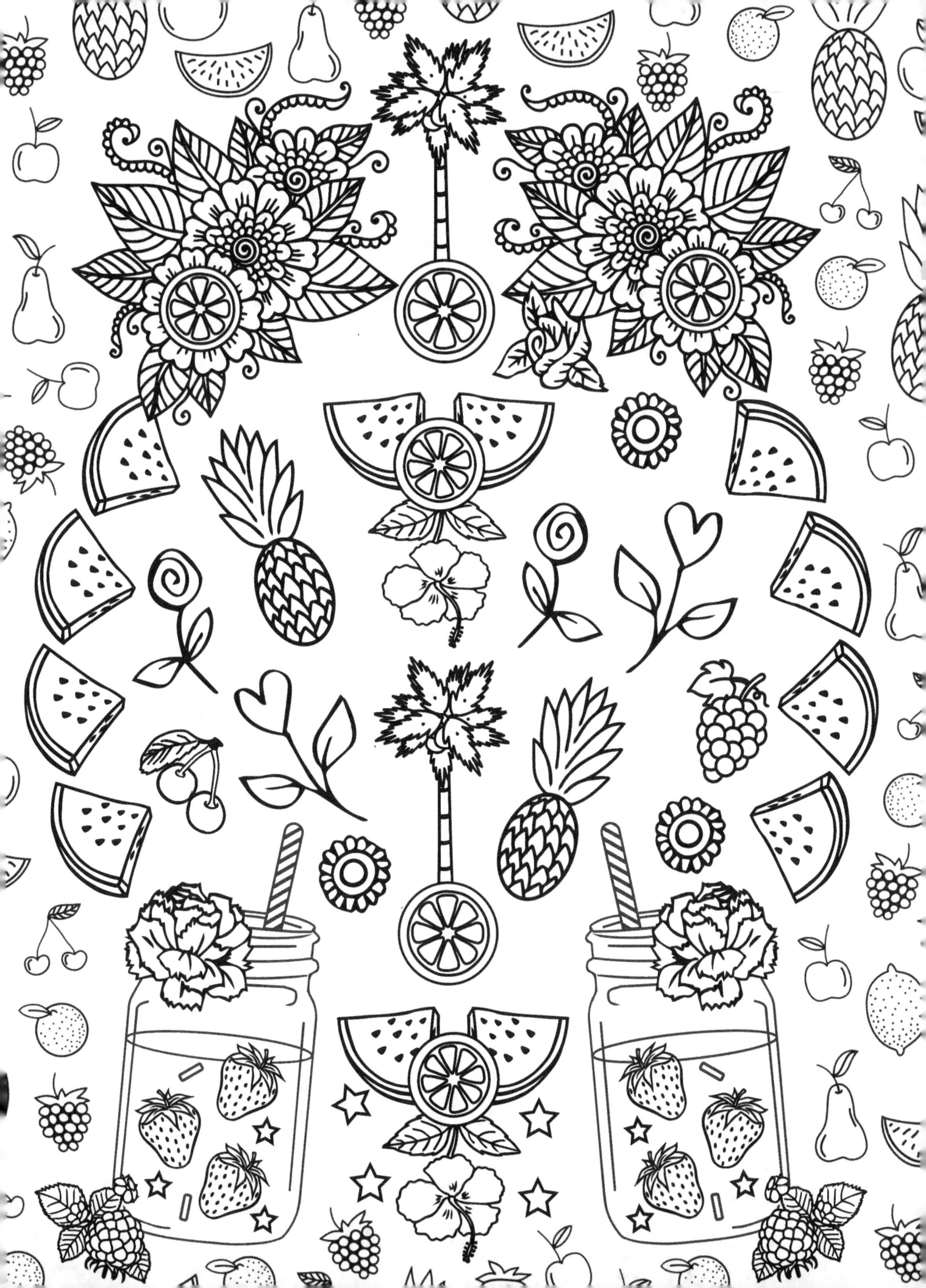

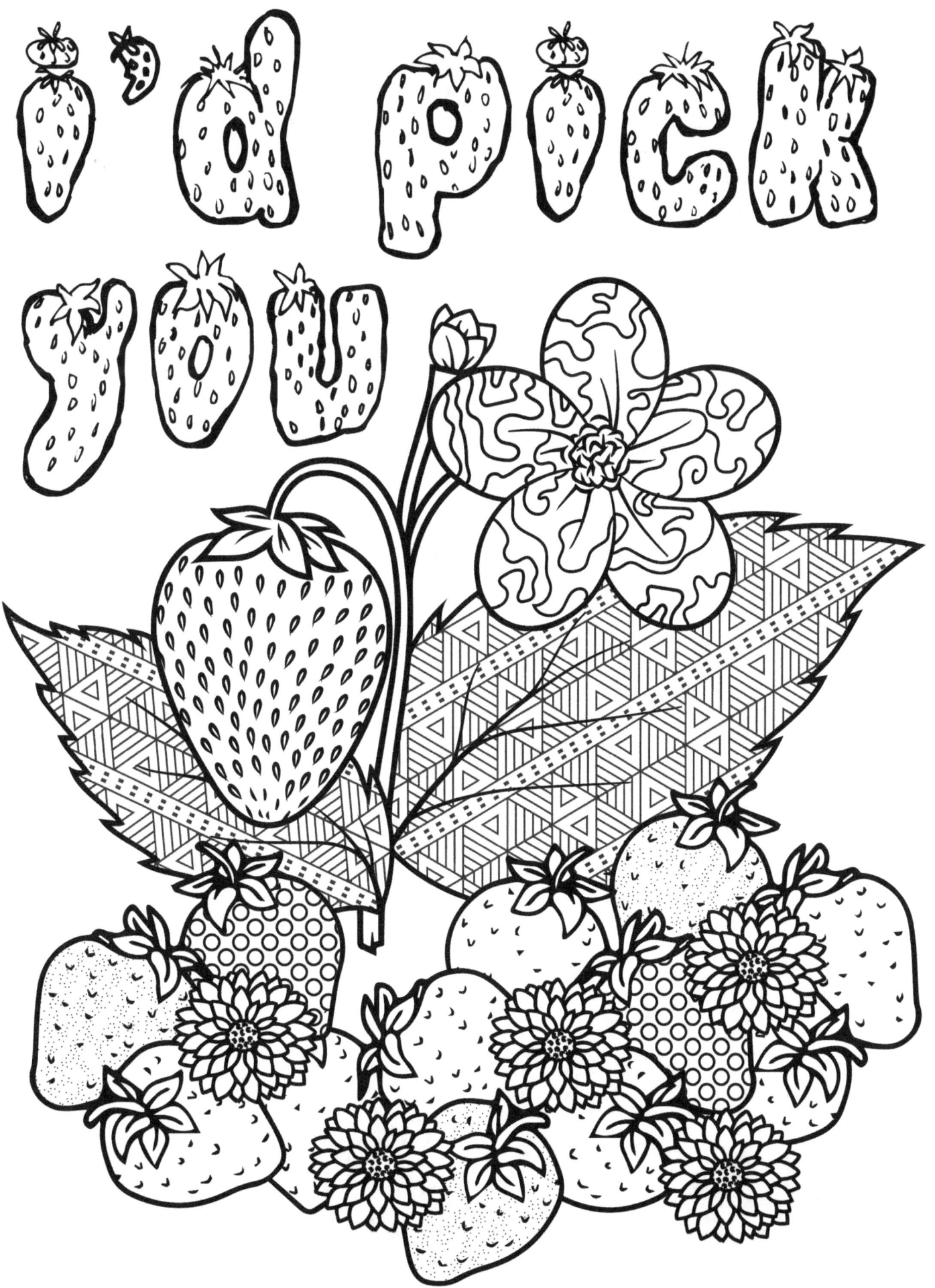

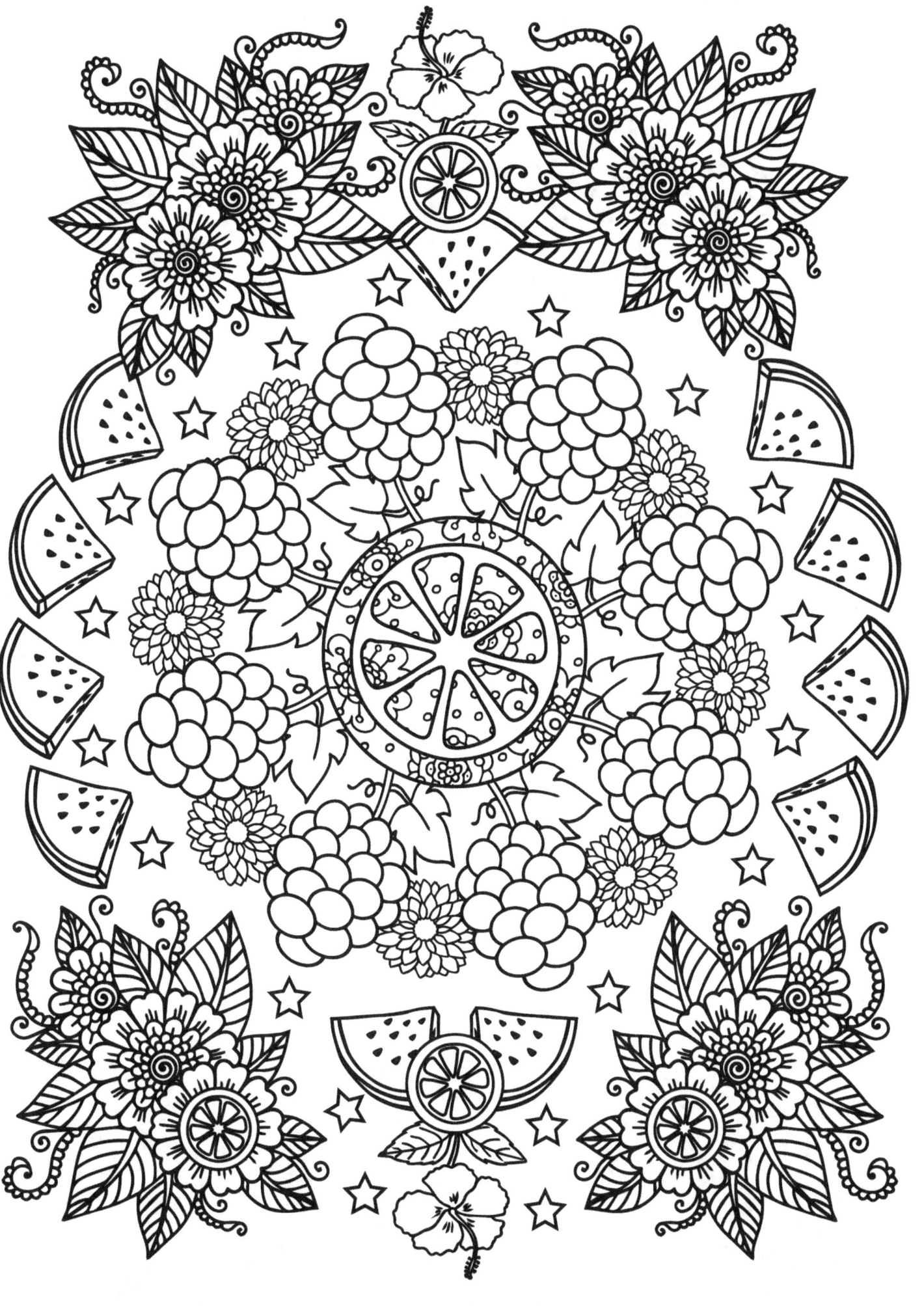

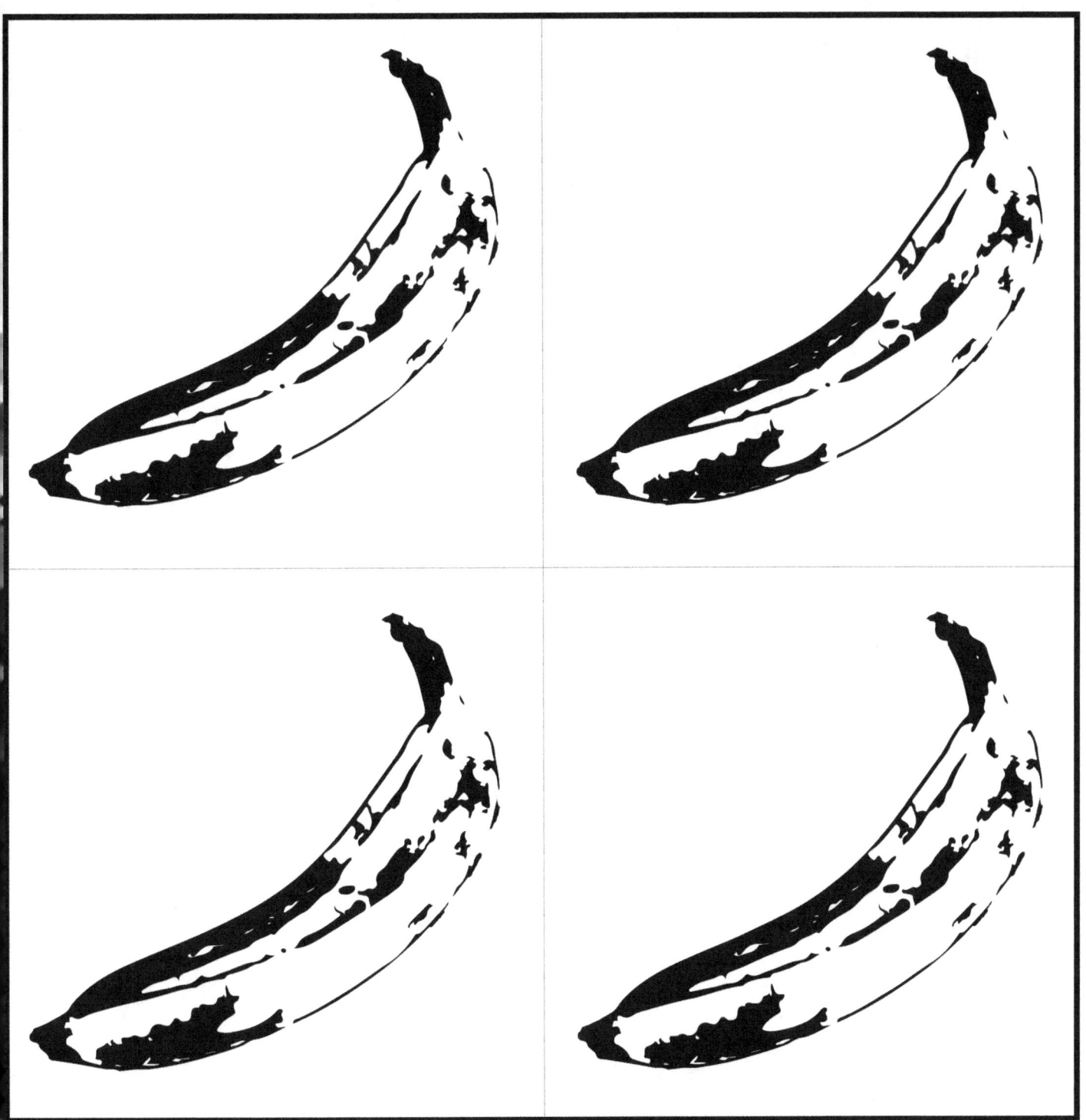

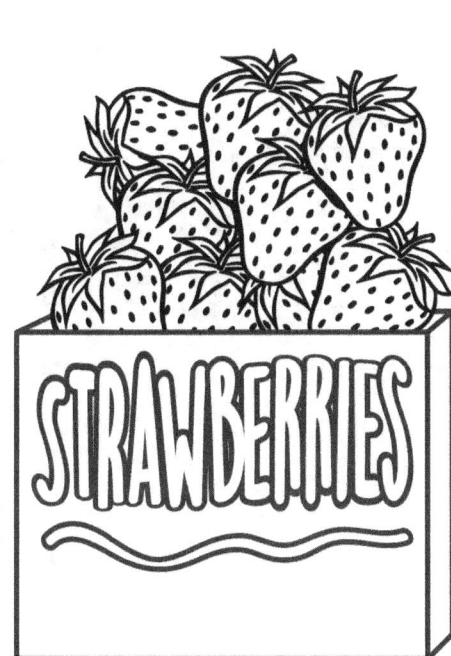

STRAWBERRIES

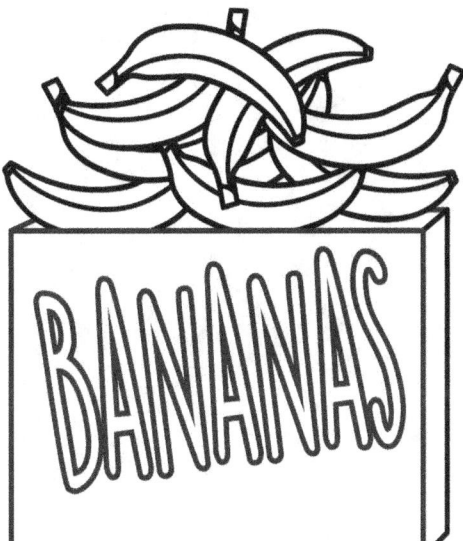

BANANAS

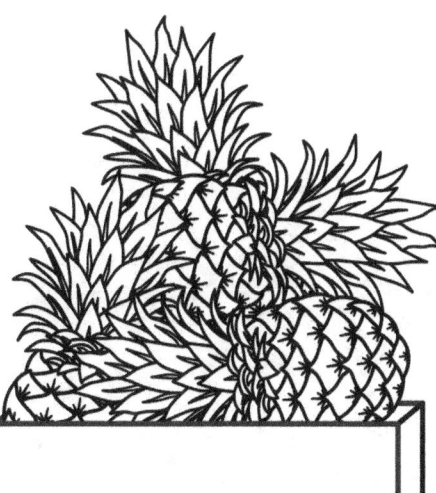

PINEAPPLES

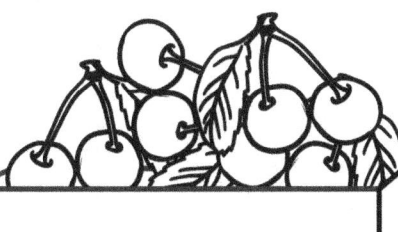

CHERRIES

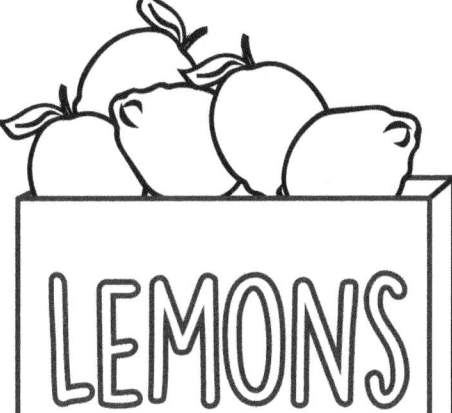

LEMONS

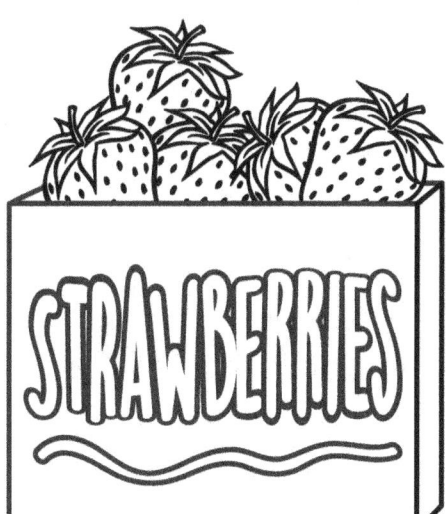

STRAWBERRIES

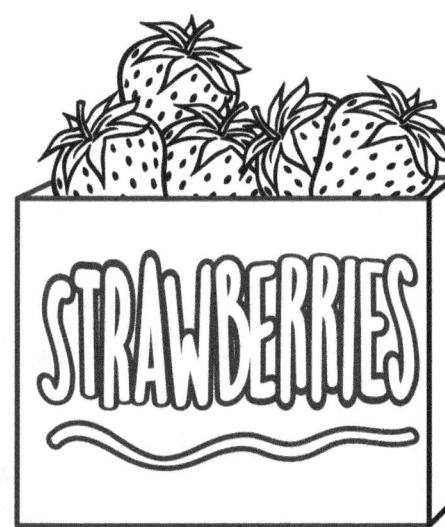

STRAWBERRIES

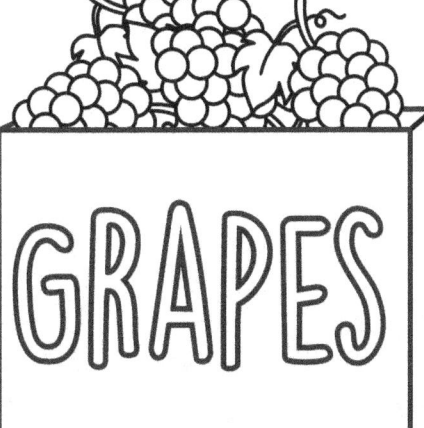

GRAPES

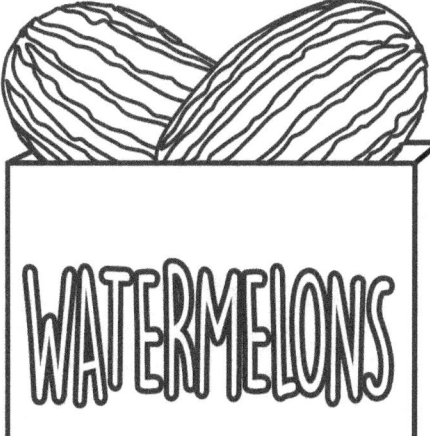

WATERMELONS